C000262745

WIGAN

FIFTY GOLDEN YEARS

A PICTORIAL HISTORY TO CELEBRATE
THE QUEEN'S JUBILEE

WIGAN
FIFTY GOLDEN YEARS

A PICTORIAL HISTORY TO CELEBRATE
THE QUEEN'S JUBILEE

The voice of Wigan for 148 years

DB
PUBLISHING

irst published in Great Britain byThe Breedon Books Publishing Company Limited
Breedon House, 44 Friar Gate, Derby, DE1 1DA. 1999

This paperback edition published in Great Britain in 2015 by DB Publishing, an imprint of
JMD Media Ltd

© Wigan Observer, 2002

All Rights Reserved. No part of this publication may be reproduced, stored in a retrieval system,
or transmitted in any form, or by any means, electronic, mechanical, photocopying,
recording or otherwise without the prior permission in writing of the copyright holders, nor
be otherwise circulated in any form or binding or cover other than in which it is published
and without a similar condition being imposed on the subsequent publisher.

ISBN 978-1-78091-503-6

Contents

A special thank you to Len Hudson at
Wigan Metro Council Archives Department
for his help and loan of pictures
in the production of this book.

Introduction

SIFTING through the archives of the *Wigan Observer* is like taking a step back in time. History jumps out from page after page of the dusty files – moments captured forever by our photographers.

It is difficult to decide which photographs best reflect the people and the town of Wigan, there are so many to choose from five decades. But we have picked out over 400 photographs – happy, sad, tragic, funny and evocative images each telling their own tale, each triggering different emotions in different people.

Flick through these pages and you may well see people and places you remember. Some of the buildings are no longer standing and many of the areas have changed quite considerably.

Yet each image provides a distinct memory of a place or a time. Wigan has changed considerably in the past 50 years. Its main industries of textiles and mining have all but disappeared. In their place is a new hi-tech Wigan designed to see it develop and thrive in the 21st century.

However, some of the town's best-known firms have survived – William Santus, the makers of Uncle Joe's Mintballs, and Heinz among them. They exist alongside the new companies which are changing the image and the industrial face of the town.

Wigan's sporting heritage has also changed. Gone are the old rugby and soccer grounds, Central and Springfield Parks, to be succeeded by the impressive JJB Stadium.

These pages also pay tribute to other sporting triumphs of which the town can be rightly proud, in the fields of swimming and athletics, to name just two.

But it is not just the famous who are celebrated here. The real people of Wigan, young and old, are what makes the town what it is today. They too deserve to be recognised and they duly take their place in this particular history book.

Some of the young faces you see in the Walks of Witness are grown now and their own children are continuing a tradition which has survived into the modern age. The older faces of those at work – or taking time out of the factories for their annual holidays – hark back to a very different way of life. Yet were those yearly trips to Blackpool any less exciting for our forefathers than the intercontinental holidays we take today?

Let's hope readers gain as much enjoyment from this book, as we had researching it!

The Changing Face

'Spite Row' in front of St Wilfred's Church.

The centre of Wigan looking down Standishgate in the 1950s.

Plenty of bygone transport to enjoy in this view of Standishgate.

The mock Tudor style of Wigan's town centre buildings, pictured here in the 1950s, is one of the hallmarks of the town.

A view from the top of Wallgate *c.*1960, showing the Dog and Partridge public house and the Wigan 5C bus.

Standishgate in the 1950s.

Wigan's cobbled
Market Square in
the 1950s with the
Hope Street
Congregational
Church rising in
the background.

The Notre Dame
Girls' School,
better known as
The Convent, on
Standishgate.

Commercial Yard, off Wigan town centre, was a popular walkway between the Market Place and Market Street. This picture was taken in the mid-1960s.

Scholes flats under construction. In the background can be seen the floodlights of Central Park.

A look back to the days when the Corporation buses were a familiar sight in Wigan as was the policeman on point duty at the top of Library Street.

Lower Scholes in the 1960s with Acton House residential home to the left and the now demolished 'upside down' houses to the back.

This man has just climbed up Birkett Street, Wigan.

Windswept and rain-soaked but still a good playground for local children ...Wells Street in the 1960s.

Wigan Market
Square in the
early 1970s.

A 1970s view of
the now-
demolished
Horseshoe
Hotel near
Scholes flats.

The Park Hotel on Wigan Market Square.

The old Town Hall in
Wigan.

Regent Street, Wigan, in the late 1960s, at the start of the slum clearance.

The Legs of Man Hotel, Wigan.

Wigan Fair on the Market Square.

The last fair on the Market
Square was this one, in 1967.

On the left can be seen the Hippodrome Theatre, Wigan.

The Court Cinema, Wigan, in 1973.

The Palace Cinema
at Ashton.

A view from the bottom of
Library Street in the mid-1950s,
before the Pavilion Cinema was
demolished to make way for the
Wigan International Swimming
Pool.

Wigan Market Place in the early 1950s.

Greenough Street in the 1960s.

A scene from the former outside market in Wigan with Cyril Barlow of Laurel Nurseries, Hindley. The rear of British Home Stores is in the background.

The Market Square in the early 1970s.

Inside Wigan's old Market Hall, now demolished.

The Market Hall in the 1980s.

The Market Hall in the 1980s.

The exterior of the old market.

In the 1960s, Wigan Market Hall was alive with the bustle of shoppers.

The Market Arcade, better known as the 'Little' Arcade, pictured here in the early 1970s.

Evidence of Marks & Spencer's original Wigan store in the Makinson Arcade, exposed again in 1974.

The old 'Little' Arcade featured the popular Gorner's Café.

Arcade shopping in the 1970s. The Market Arcade, better known as the 'Little' Arcade with (below) the Makinson Arcade.

The Makinson Arcade pictured in 1985.

Lowes store in the Market Place. It was demolished in the 1980s.

The 1980s were a time of much change in Wigan town centre. This 1986 photograph captures the end of an era and the promise of new days ahead. Note the much-loved Park Hotel, the fittings from which are now part of the Wigan Pier Heritage Centre.

Wigan's Frog Lane Hospital.

Wigan Infirmary in 1979.

Wigan Casino's heyday as a home for Northern Soul music was the mid-1970s.

A view from the balcony of Wigan Casino.

Wigan Casino caught fire in March 1982 while empty and the extensive damage saw the club demolished some days later.

Demolition begins at
Wigan Casino after the
disastrous fire.

Hindley Green railway
station in its heyday with
its name spelled out in
flowers.

Hindley railway station in 1975.

Wigan Central railway station in the early 1960s.

Wigan Central railway station in 1964 based, not surprisingly, in Station Road.

Gathurst Bridge under construction in 1959. One man was killed during the building of the bridge which spanned the railway line and canal.

Wigan's International Swimming Pool being built.

The canal at Parbold.

Haigh Canal in the bleak midwinter.

Haigh Windmill sets off this already picturesque scene.

Lil's Café, Preston Road, Standish.

Wigan's Mesnes Park, pictured from the clock tower of the former grammar school in the 1950s.

A ploughing match at Billinge in the 1980s.

Not much of a view… a local resident looks over her garden fence to the slag tips at Ince.

The demolition of Wigan RL's Central Park in September 1999.

The same year and Wigan Athletic's Springfield Park suffers the same fate. Of course, both rugby league and soccer clubs now play at the splendid JJB Stadium.

Changing political arena… the first meeting of the Wigan Metropolitan Council in 1974.

Happy Days

Happy Wiganers about to depart by coach for their annual holiday at Torquay. This and the following pictures were taken in July 1967.

These young lads-about-town are ready to catch their train to start their holiday.

Waving goodbye at
Wigan railway station.

With bucket and
spade at the ready this
young man is ready
for the seaside – and
he appears to have a
privileged seat on the
bus taking him there.

Youngsters pose for the camera before the train arrives to take them, who knows where? The seaside perhaps, or maybe a day trip to London.

And here it comes. A holiday train steams into Wigan station and the scramble for seats is about to begin.

Holidaymakers await their coach in Market Street.

On a sunny day 50 years ago, Wigan pensioners pose with the Mayor of Wigan on the Market Square before an annual day trip to the seaside.

Didn't we have a lovely time, the day we went to Blackpool in the 1960s?

We're off to Wembley! Workers of Lord & Sharman slipper works prepare to watch Wigan RL in 1960.

Coops sewing factory workers pictured at Wallgate Station in the 1950s.

Coops employees off to Blackpool in the mid-1950s.

Former Coops employees arriving at Blackpool in 1957.

Leah Clark and her husband Walter, who was the drummer at the Empress Ballroom, Wigan, where this photograph was taken.

Wigan Gilbert and Sullivan Society pictured before rehearsals for *The Gondoliers.*

Standish Band go Christmas caroling in 1958.

Youngsters from Smalley Street and Collingwood Street line up before a street party.

It's hard work but these youngster still seem to be enjoying picking potatoes in the Garwsood area in the 1970s.

Bird Street residents Liz Ramsdale, Enid Keates and Sylvia Armstrong were off to Las Vegas in 1997, in the company of Caroline Aherne after appearing regularly on her *Mrs Merton* television show.

The bride's mum sheds a tear as her daughter ties the knot at a mock wedding at All Saints School at Appley Bridge.

A trip for pupils and staff of Mere Oaks School in the summer of 1975.

A May Queen charity cheque is presented to Dr Phillip Silver.

Youngsters enjoy donkey rides at Haigh Hall in the 1970s.

Local Morris dancers raised money for charity.

It's 1957 and this young man is a student at Wigan Mining and Technology College. The bike is a Douglas Dragonfly.

Boys Brigade drill… with a difference.

Leaders on a Boys Brigade training course.

Wigan ABC cinemagoers pictured with projectionist Marlow Bradshaw.

A night to remember at a Heinz dance at the Court Hall.

A tearful moment at a Remembrance Day parade in the late 1980s.

Pigeon fancier Harry Bates pictured with some of his feathered friends.

Wrightington Hospital
annual garden fete in June
1979.

A typical May Queen group.

Wigan parish choir on top of the church on Ascension Day morning.

The Mayor of Wigan with local children in fancy dress.

Wigan Boys' Club band at rehearsal in 1965.

Wigan May Queen in 1964.

Members of Wigan Ladies Circle at a presentation at a local restaurant in the 1960s.

The undie taker... a cheeky chappie at Wigan Carnival in the 1990s.

Land ahoy! A Wigan boat rally in 1983.

Working Days

A rag and bone cart trundles over the canal bridge on Pottery Road.

Fruiterer with his horse and cart on his rounds in Wigan in the 1950s.

Window cleaner James Edwards of Atherton Road in the 1950s. The advertisement on his cart assured customers that he was fully insured.

A postman takes his four-legged pal to work in the 1960s.

Cable jointer Vernon Jackson takes a well-earned lunch break.

Refuse collectors hard at work in 1967 in Wallgate.

Teddy Lea of Marshall Lane outside the joinery shop in Marsh Green in 1957.

The last steam train at Wigan Central Station with left, George Hilton (guard), Donald Hodgson (driver) and Tony Dirkin (fireman) on 2 November 1964.

Always popular, Wigan's Mesnes Park café had a more elegant atmosphere when this photograph was taken almost half a century ago.

A local family take the weight off their feet at Wigan Baths' Café.

Wigan Central Lending Library in the late 1950s.

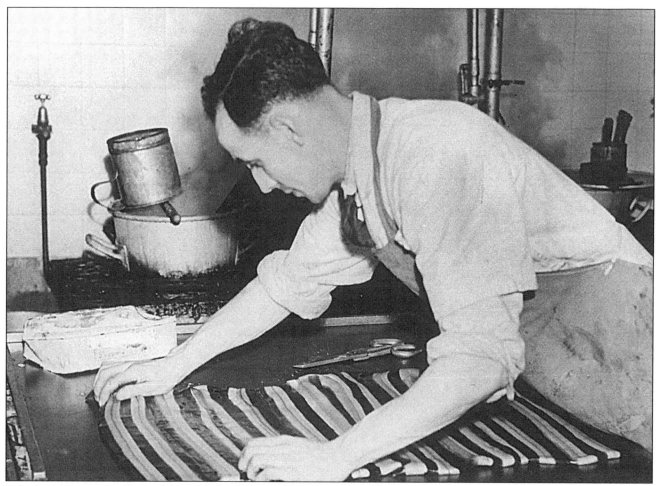

Mint humbug production at the Santus factory in Wigan in the early 1950s.

Ladies of the Santus sweet stall in Wigan market.

Print day at the *Wigan Observer* in the 1950s.

Compositers at the *Wigan Observer* making up pages in the days of hot metal newspaper production in the 1970s.

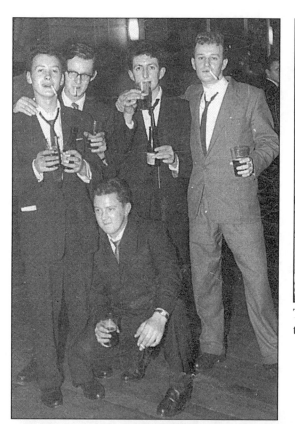

These young Wigan men are celebrating a National Service posting to the exotic delights of Hong Kong in 1959.

Far from home… Carole Burns of the Women's Royal Army Corps in Hong Kong in January 1972.

A young hod carrier working on the Norley Hall estates nearly half a century ago.

Apprentice joiner John Brennan at work on the Norley Hall shops in 1957.

The year is 1958 and two concrete layers are working on the shops and flats at Norley Hall.

Cotton mill girls take a break.

Redundant workers face a bleak future as it is announced that another cotton mill is to close in Ince.

A visit from the Mayor of Wigan at Enfield Mill, Pemberton, in June 1954.

A hive of activity… Coops sewing factory in the 1950s.

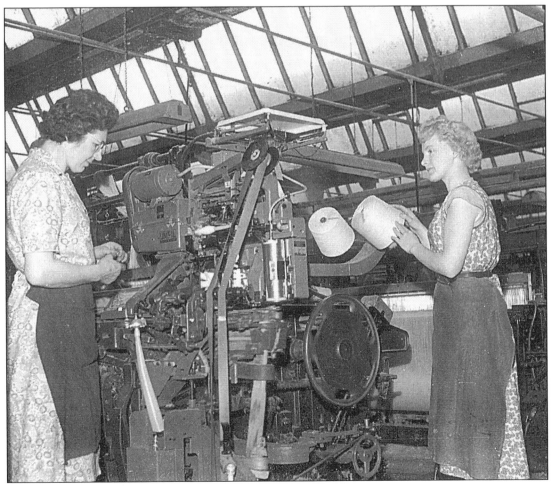

Preparing the bobbins at a Wigan cotton mill in 1960.

Women at work at Coops sewing factory.

These girls from Rappaport's sewing factory at Ince are seen on the eve of a colleagues' wedding. The bride-to-be was festooned and led through the streets by workmates.

Clocking-off for the last time… with the gift of a clock. A presentation to a long-serving employee at Turner's-TBA at Hindley Green in the 1960s.

Production line at the Tupperware factory at Beech Hill, Wigan.

Retirement presentation to spinner Polly Woods, on stage in the canteen of Trencherfield Mill in the 1950s.

Staff at the Heinz factory at Standish enjoy a party before the factory closes.

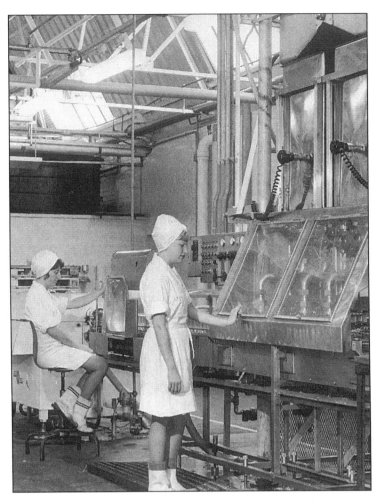

The pickling department at De Hann (Foods) Ltd in June 1961.

Pickling department at the Heinz factory at Kitt Green.

A group of boys, aged about 15, training for the mines at Wigan Junction pit in 1953. Behind them is Trencherfield Mill.

NCB trainees at Clayton Street School, Wigan, in early 1955.

One of the last shifts at the now-demolished Parkside Colliery.

Pemberton Colliery in May 1985.

Golborne Colliery in the 1980s.

Cars parked outside Bickershaw Colliery.

Striking miners and their supporters march through the centre of Wigan in 1984.

Miller's Autoservices showing off their range in the 1950s.

Cars parked outside A & B
Motors, Wigan, in the 1960s.

Proud owners of a new car at a Wigan showroom in the 1950s.

Remembered with great affection is James Berry (seen on the right, presenting a trophy). Mr Berry owner of the Shevington garage and car salesroom, was a great local benefactor.

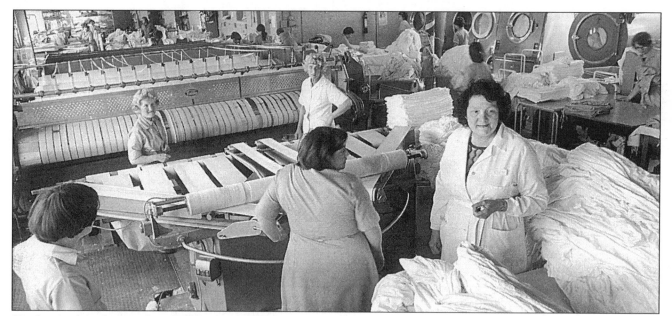

Hard at work in the laundry of Billinge Hospital.

The laundry at Wigan Baths.

This little shop on Bridgewater Street, Hindley, has long been demolished along with the surrounding houses.

Harriet Parr in her grocer's shop on old Bridge Street, Hindley, in the 1950s.

Are you being served? Manageress Irene Jackson with her assistants at the Lancashire and Cheshire Rubber Company in Market Street, Wigan.

Staff at the Louis Fisher store in Wigan.

May Day Rally in 1953. In the centre is Gerry Kennan, small of stature but big of heart. When George Orwell came to Wigan in 1936 he visited Kennan's house in Beech Hill and it was he who showed Orwell the pockets of Wigan poverty.

Pickets at Wigan Infirmary during industrial action in 1982.

Marks & Spencer's staff at Wigan at a social gathering around 1958.

Hello caller... Wigan telephone exchange.

Wigan police officers with their new Panda cars in 1967.

Staff at Pennington's furniture store, Millgate, Wigan.

A student on a building course at Wigan Tech poses with his trendy new scooter in 1958.

Members of Wigan Junior Chamber of Commerce outside Wigan Baths in July 1969.

Back to School

A group from Britannia Bridge Girls' School in 1952.

Another 1952 group from Britannia Bridge Girls' School. Back row (left to right): Irene Hudson, Eunice Lloyd, Betty Foster, Sheila McCarthy, Eileen Lowton, Hilda Banks, Lilian Speakman. Middle row: Betty Unsworth, Lillian Aspinall, Joyce Kyte, Sandra Brabbin, Hilda Santus, Audrey McAllister, Julie Holding. Front row: Dorothy Fletcher, Elsie Bird, Marjorie Winstanley, Mona Tymon, June Ashton, Jean Marsden, D. Fitzsimmons, Winnie Hilda Evans, Eileen Murphy.

Girls of Notre Dame High School, Wigan, 1952.

Standish Lower Ground Church of
England School, 1952.

Girls of St Patrick's, Hardy Butts, 1953.

Mrs Brown's class of 1955 at Sacred Heart School, Springfield.

Senior Class II of Ashton Secondary Modern School, 1956.

Class group of 1957 from St Andrew's Junior School.

Teacher and pupils of Thomas
Linacre School, May 1960.

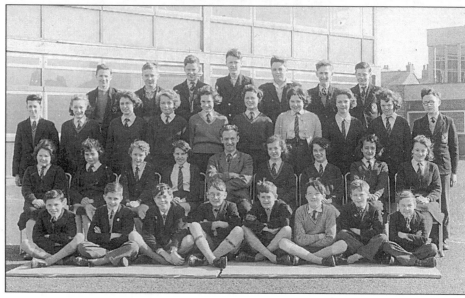

Abraham Guest School pupils
and teacher in the early 1960s.

Teacher and pupils of Thomas Linacre School, May 1963.

The Mayor and Mayoress, Councillor and Mrs Bob Lyon, become honorary members of the Tufty Club in the early 1970s.

Mesnes High School pupils felt strongly enough about one particular issue in 1976 that they staged a 'demo'.

It's perhaps difficult for modern-day pupils, used to computers on their desks, to appreciate just how basic were the facilities in Wigan's schools not all that long ago.

Councillor George Macdonald, Mayor of Wigan in 1976, joins pupils from a local school in a charity collection.

The safe cyclists of Hawkley Hall Middle School who received their cycling proficiency certificates from PC Roy Edgar (left) the accident prevention officer for Wigan, and (right) Inspector Chris Rattigan.

Pupils at a Wigan school queue for their dinners.

Hindley Green School pupils enjoy their break-time snacks.

Standish High School staff in 1978.

Standish High School canteen staff in 1978.

In 1979 the biology laboratory at Upholland High School was unveiled.

Prize Day at St Thomas More High School in 1983.

Studying hard in the library of St Thomas More High School in 1984.

Pupils of St John's CE School, Pemberton, in 1984.

This is how it's done… local schoolchildren receiving basketball coaching in 1984.

Dr Phillip Silver receives a cheque for his fund for Cancer Research from the sixth form of St John Rigby School in 1978.

Students at Upholland College in 1984.

Standish High School choir in the 1980s.

Edgar Wrigglesworth, the teacher who introduced computers to Wigan schools.

St Thomas More School's under-12s cricket team.

St Thomas More School's under-13s cricket team.

Pupils from Bryn Gates County Primary School present a cheque to the Dr Barnardos organisation.

Youngsters from Elim Pentecostal School hold a teddy bears' picnic in November 1985.

Pupils from Woodfield Primary School present a cheque to the NSPCC in 1985.

Young soccer stars from Bryn St Peter's in 1985.

Hope Special School receive £300 raised by pupils from the former Whitley High School in 1986.

A break from lessons as these Wigan schoolchildren enjoy a nature ramble in May 1985.

Netball stars from Castle Hill School, Hindley, in 1985.

Young sportsmen from Woodfold Primary School with their trophies in 1988.

Students from Cansfield High School present a charity cheque in 1988.

Pupils and staff from Byrchall High School present a charity cheque in 1988.

Mayhem, Mishaps, Disasters

On 18 March 1979, the pit village of Golborne was changed forever. A methane gas explosion brought terror to the mine – eventually killing ten men. As shocked workers took in the scale of the disaster, NUM leader Joe Gormley and Industry Secretary Tony Benn visited the scene of the disaster.

Left: NUM boss Joe Gormley meets Golborne pitmen.

Below: Industry Secretary Tony Benn listens as miners share their frightening experience

Above and right: Stunned miners end their shift at Golborne.

Subdued miners waiting for the cage for the first shift back after the 1979 disaster at Golborne Colliery..

Flooding under the railway bridge at Newtown in 1954 – still a major stumbling block to a free-flowing traffic system at The Saddle junction.

Flooding at Higher Ince in 1954.

Mrs Sylvia Brazendale is not enjoying a seaside paddle but showing the depth of the floodwater in the garden of her Wigan home in 1969.

Appley Bridge floods in the 1980s.

Appley Bridge floods in the 1980s.

Flooding in Wigan causes chaos for motorists.

A flooded road in Shevington in the 1980s.

This runaway donkey led everyone a merry dance through the streets of Wigan.

Captured! The runaway is reunited with its owners.

Muddied heroes from the local fire brigade serve up a good feed to hungry horse Samra after rescuing the pregnant mare from a swamp.

A cat is stranded after running up a concrete lamp-post on Woodhouse Lane.

Concerned local residents hold a blanket under the descending cat in case it slips and then a passing van driver comes to the rescue.

Police examine the wreckage after a car crashed into a lamp-post in 1983.

An overturned private motor car, in 1977.

Firemen with cutting equipment free the body of the driver of a lorry which crashed off the M6 viaduct and into the River Douglas at Gathurst in the late 1980s.

A lorry is wrecked after coming off the M6 viaduct at Gathurst in 1974. The driver escaped with leg injuries.

And then the lorry is hauled back on to the M6 motorway.

The chimney at Giants Hall Colliery is demolished in 1972.

Above: A view from Westwood of the first cooling tower being blown up at Westwood power station in 1989.
Below: A view from Highfield of the second tower being blown up.

The huge fire which ripped through the Ruberoid factory at Appley Bridge on 12 June 2000.

A portent of disaster? The Hale-Bopp comet in the night sky over Wigan Parish Church in March 1997.

Sporting Days

Ringside seats at Central Park in the 1950s.

October 1957 saw the arrival of Mick Sullivan to Wigan RL, greeted here by Billy Boston and Eric Ashton. Sully enjoys his first sausage, bacon and eggs, Wigan's customary meal after training.

Another big crowd at Central Park, this time in 1960. The Douglas Stand, with its rooftop press box, was demolished and rebuilt in 1973.

Billy Boston leads out Wigan for his last game for the club, in 1968.

Action at Central Park.

Football coaching at the Police Athletic Ground in 1957. Ray Marshall (Southport) and Roy Kilner (Lancashire Amateurs) were the tutors.

Wigan Athletic manager Les Rigby acknowledges the Latics fans after the club reached the 1973 FA Trophy Final, where they lost 2-1 to Scarborough.

Skipper Ian Gillibrand, followed by goalkeeper John Brown, leads out Wigan Athletic at Hereford in August 1978, for the Latics' first game in the Football League after being elected to the Fourth Division.

Pictured in this display team from the early 1950s are (standing, left to right): Bunny Jinks, Bert Mellor, John Whiteside, Eric Cranston and Frank Yeo. At the front are Dennis Wilson and Ted Hornby.

Lads from the Beef It Gym, Hindley, showing their muscles.

Members of Goose Green Pigeon Club at a prize awards evening in 1958.

A 1950s presentation evening of the Navigation Fishing Club, Gathurst.

It is 1965 and members of
Appley Bridge Fishing Club pose
with their trophies.

A bowls team from the Melverley Street bus depot of Wigan Corporation Transport Dept, probably in the late 1950s or
early 60s.

The Mayor opens the new bowls season at Wigan Subscription Bowling Club in 1966.

Grass track racing at Wigan around 1967.

Ken Saxon from Scholes, pictured on his BSA motorbike in 1958.

Pete Williams with a triple engined Norton on which he tried to break the motorbike land speed record.

Olympic athlete Daley Thompson at the old Robin Park in the early 1990s.

Wigan road races in 1977.

Hindley athlete David Grindley with the bronze medal which he won in the 4 x 400 men's relay event at the Barcelona Olympics in 1992.

Wigan Wasps Olympic hopefuls are (from left to right) Steve Poulter, Nick Hodson and Martin Smith, and Annabelle Cripps, Gaynor Stanley, Ann Osgerby and June Croft.

Diving in at Wigan International Pool in July 1968.

Wiganers flocked to the newly-opened swimming pool.

Wigan Wasps are on the road, photographed outside Wigan International Pool before setting off to compete.

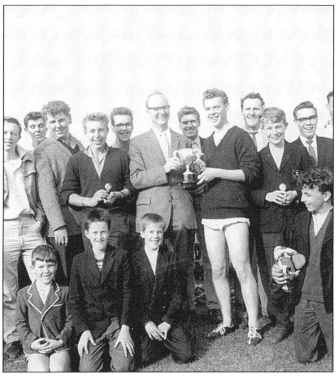

Wigan's education officer John Fielding presents the trophies after a local athletics match in 1959.

Swimmers at Ashton Leisure Centre in July 1985.

Wigan Observer ten-pin bowlers at Leigh Bowl.

Young cricketers at
Bull Hey in the
1970s.

Sports day at Wigan
Grammar School in
1957.

Woodhouse Stadium in the 1970s, home of local schools' sports days.

Canoeist Graeme Thomas leads with David Sedgewick not far behind in July 1984.

The charge of the little brigade. Romans versus Barbarians kids football match at Robin Park in 1994.

Back in Fashion

A Pendlebury's fashion parade in 1953.

Material girls: ladies choosing fabrics in Pendlebury's.

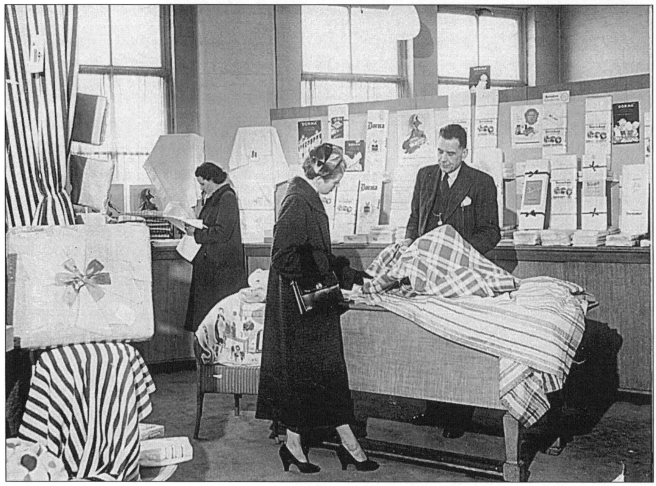

A model chats to the audience at a Spirella fashion show at the New Court Ballroom.

The audience at a spring fashion show at the New Court Ballroom in the 1960s.

Right and bottom left: Models from a fashion show at the All Saints Secondary School in 1967.

Right: Sporting a natty line in Easter bonnets, former Miss United Kingdom and Miss World runner-up Kathleen Winstanley cuts a silk ribbon to open a new boutique in Castle Hill, Hindley.

Mini marvels – late-night revellers at Wigan Casino in the 1960s.

Lucky chap! Mayor of Wigan, Councillor Bob Lyons, with contestants at a Parkside Colliery Queen Final.

Spots, squares and flowers are themes for these ladies at an event in 1974, with Councillor Lyons, then Mayor of Wigan, in attendance.

Towering ambition: students get to grips with the latest craze – platform shoes – in 1975.

High heels. A
student wears
platform boots
as she studies.

Charity
walking in Bay
City Rollers
gear at Wigan
Infirmary,
*c.*1975.

Tank tops, kipper ties and floral shirts are the order of the day for these youngsters in 1975.

More 1970s fashion as these young people meet the Mayor and Mayoress, Councillor and Mrs Tom Morgan, in 1975.

Cool dudes at Shevington Youth Club in 1979.

Gillian Smith and Lesley Hamilton become the first punk rock panto dames, in the St Aidan's Christmas play in 1979.

Parkas are in evidence at Shevington Youth Club in 1979.

Leotards were practical when it came to doing aerobics in the 1980s.

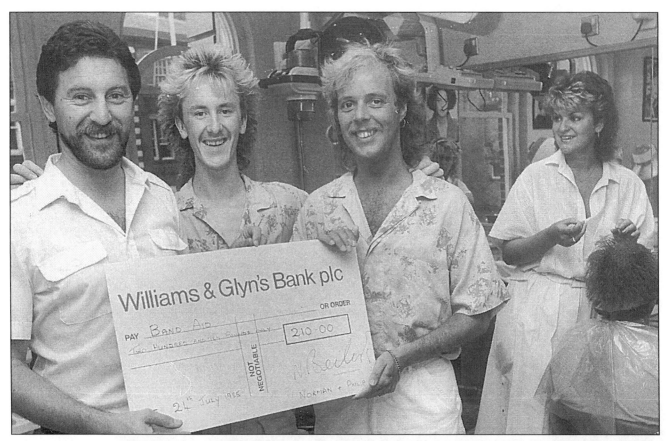

Stylists from
Norman &
Philip present a
cheque to the
Band Aid
charity in 1985.

Line-up of Miss
Wigan finalists
in 1984.

And they were just as lovely for the Miss Wigan of 1985.

Striped jumpers seem to be in vogue with some members of this 1986 ladies darts team.

Mullets to the fore in this 1986 group!

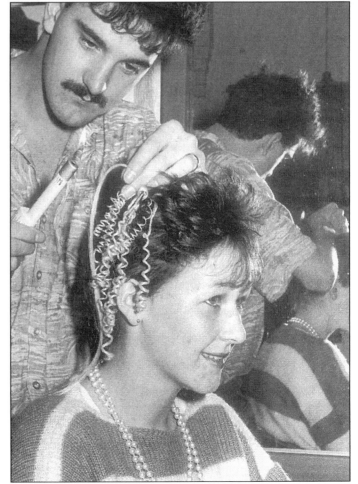

Norman & Philip stylists Carolyn Barnett and Paul Kirkham let new styles go to their heads!

Musical Interludes

Bring on the Boys – Beatles fans waiting for the concert to begin at the Ritz in October 1964.

Waiting for their heroes. The Beatles concerts in October 1964 came very early on a nationwide tour.

Marc Bolan of T-Rex at the Ritz in November 1971.

Marc Bolan fans close to the stage at the November 1971 concert.

Peace, man! Camping out at the 1972 Bickershaw Festival.

Donovan on stage at the 1972 Bickershaw Festival.

Hippies young and old at the Bickershaw Festival.

Fans brave the lashing rain at the 1972 Bickershaw Festival.

Carl Palmer of Emerson, Lake and Palmer at the Ritz in the mid-1970s.

Wigan Casino regulars take to the floor.

Wigan Casino all-nighters in the mid-1970s.

This Wigan Youth Club band of the late 1970s were called Condemned.

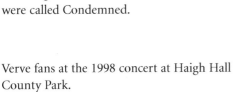

Verve fans at the 1998 concert at Haigh Hall County Park.

An aerial view showing the huge crowd at the Haigh Hall concert.

More Verve fans at Haigh Hall, apparently cheering for the camera.

This Verve fan seems to be drinking it all in.

Huge screens either side of the stage magnify singer Richard Ashcroft, during the Verve's 1998 concert.

Pop band Oasis shoot new video in Wigan.

Noel and Liam with the rest of the Oasis band during the shoot for the new single.

Right: Back where he belongs! Verve's lead singer Richard Ashcroft performs live in front of his hometown crowd.

Young and Old

The 7th Wigan (All Saints') Scout group off to Stafford in 1952. The lorry was paid for by the Scouts collecting 10,000 jam jars and selling them for a penny each to raise approximately £42.

An impromptu game of cricket at Poolstock in the 1950s.

The labels on their jackets give away their secret: these youngsters from a Pemberton club are off on their annual day trip in the summer of 1962. The Mayor of Wigan, Councillor Thomas Monks, is there to see them off.

Children and their mums at Wrightington Fish Pond in the 1960s.

An ice cream van attracts young customers in the 1960s.

What do we have here? These young Wiganers pose outside a terraced house. Perhaps there is a clue to be gleaned from the badge bearing a torch flame, sported by some of the youngsters.

Sledging on Ashurst Beacon in February 1969.

Local schoolchildren who watched the demolition of Giants Hall chimney play on the rubble that remained in November 1972.

Two girls from Bird Street, Ince, pictured in 1968.

Dr Philip Silver receives a cheque for his appeal from these youngsters in fancy dress.

Abram St John's Primary School pupils play in the snow in the late 1980s.

Fun and frolics at the first Haigh Carnival.

Young Wigan anglers brave the rain.

This little girl takes to the swings on a local park.

Boy Scouts raise glasses of orange juice to the Mayor of Wigan, Councillor Arnold Singer and Mrs Gladys Singer, before the start of their annual camp at Bispham Hall, Billinge, in 1966.

Scenes from the Boy Scouts annual camp at Bispham Hall, Billinge, in 1966.

More camp scenes from the Boy Scouts annual camp at Bispham Hall, Billinge, in 1966.

Ball play: families take a break at Haigh Hall.

Splashing around... these young Wiganers don wellies to enjoy the puddles.

These children are posing in Beech Hill Valley in the summer of 1977.

Youngsters at Haigh Hall Country
Park playground in 1977.

Local Brownies pictured in 1979.

Children at the Heinz Christmas party in 1985.

The 1985 Wigan Carnival and these babies and their proud mums enjoy the sunshine.

Wigan Carnival clowns in 1985.

The Mayor of Wigan, Councillor George Macdonald, is guest of honour at the Wigan & District Guards Association annual garden party.

Mayor George Macdonald at a Christmas party for senior citizens in 1976.

Councillor George Macdonald again, this time attending a community tea party in Wigan.

Local ladies display their tasty offerings at a charity sale.

Councillor Bob Lyons, Mayor of Wigan in 1975, pours the tea.

Walking Days

A policeman stands at the top of Greenough Street during the Whit Monday Walk in the Coronation year of 1953.

The banner carriers of St Andrew's School, Springfield on Walking Day 1953.

St Joseph's Whit Monday Walk in 1956.

St Patrick's Church, Walking Day 1960.

The Mayor, clergy and officials line up before taking part in a Walking Day in the 1960s.

A Mothers' Union rally at the Drill Hall in the 1960s.

Platt Lane Mission, Walking Day in the 1960s.

St Catharine's, Wigan, Walking Day in the early 1960s.

Standish Lads Boys' Brigade marching band with St Wilfrid's Church in the background.

Scarisbrick Street Baptist Church, Walking Day 1966.

St Barnabas, Marsh Green, Walking Day 1966.

St Benedict's, Hindley, Walking Day 1966.

St Elizabeth's Church, Walking Day 1966.

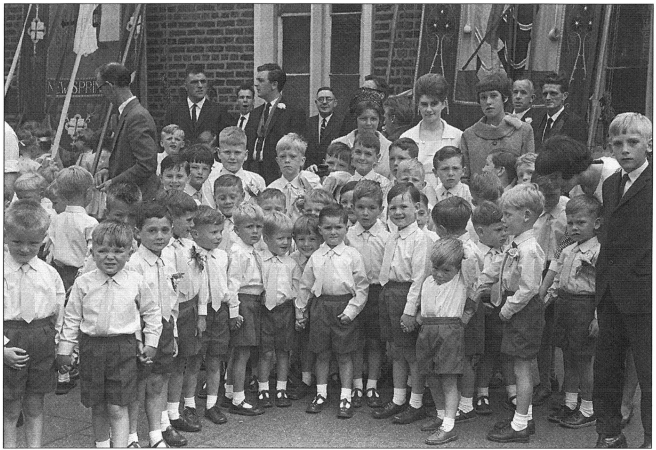

St John's Church, New Springs, Walking Day 1966.

St Thomas's Church, Walking Day 1966.

St Michael's,
Swinley, Walking
Day 1966.

Wigan Parish
Church, Walking
Day 1967.

Wigan Parish Church, Walking Day 1967.

Wigan Parish Church, Walking Day in the 1960s.

Standish Walks, 1968.

Standish Walks, 1968.

How cute! Children of St Marie's on a Walking Day.

Ladies from Birchley St Mary's Church, Walking Day 1983.

Braving the rain during the Billinge Methodist walk in 1985.

Tiny tots during the Standish St Marie's walk, 1985.

A welcome breather for these tiny choristers during the Billinge walk in 1986.

Standish Methodist Church, Walking Day 1986.

Two tiny tots take part in a Wigan Walking Day in 1986.

Best feet forward for these little girls during St Wilfrid's Walking Day at Standish in 1986.

Youngsters from All Saints' Parish Church, Walking Day 1986.

Famous Visitors

Prime Minister Harold Wilson visits Wigan in 1966.

Labour politician Denis Healey, variously Chancellor of the Exchequer and Defence Secretary, gets a word of advice from a pensioner at Higher Ince Labour Club in the 1970s.

James Callaghan, the Labour leader, visits Wigan's late MP Roger Stott at his home in Aspull in 1980.

Conservative minister Michael Hestletine at Wigan Pier before its present-day transformation.

Jeffery Archer, millionaire author and Conservative politician visits Wigan Tories in 1985, long before his disgrace and prison sentence.

Prime Minister Margaret Thatcher with Professor Graham Ashworth, Councillor Audrey Bennett, the Mayor of Wigan, and Environment Minister David Trippier. Mrs Thatcher was launching the Tidy Britain HQ at Wigan in January 1990.

Makerfield MP Ian McCartney and Jackie Best with Tony Blair when the Prime Minister visited Mr McCartney's home in Platt Bridge, Wigan, in 1995.

Round-the-world yachtsman Sir Alec Rose visits a Wigan school in 1967.

Wigan artist J. Lawrence Isherwood at work painting the portrait of a Wigan vicar.

Singer Frankie Vaughan opened a local Wigan store in 1967.

The Spinners folk group opening Dawson's music shop in Hallgate in 1967.

Entertainer Dickie Henderson opens Wigan Road service station in 1969.

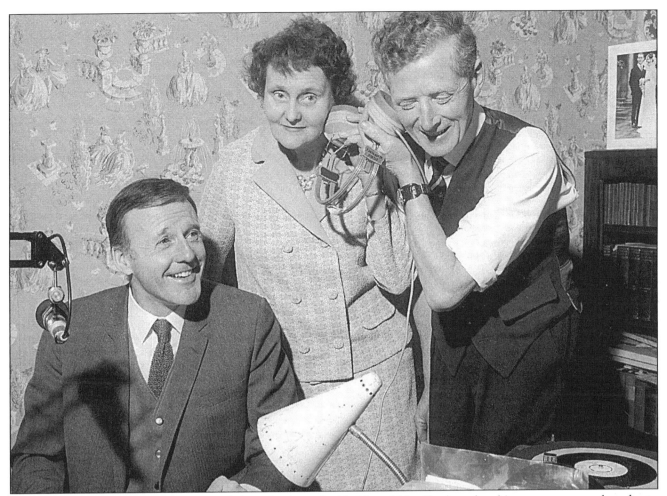

Jimmy Young, the veteran broadcaster and singer is pictured with Mr and Mrs Sharkey when his programme was broadcast from Wigan in the 1970s.

Liz Dawn, better known as *Coronation Street's* Vera Duckworth, opens a Wigan furniture store.

Violet Carson, who played Ena Sharples in *Coronation Street'*, signs autographs at Wrightington Hospital League of Friends garden party in 1978.

Clement Freud
and chairman of
Inter City, Chris
Green, sample the
product after
opening the Inter
City sandwich
shop factory in
Wigan.

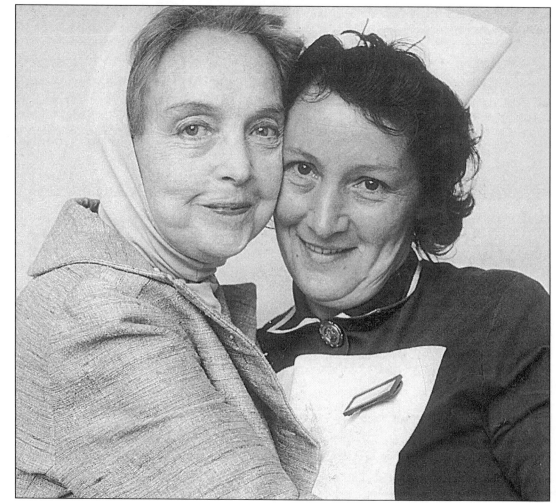

Silent movie star
Lillian Gish (left)
after her hip
operation at
Wrightington
Hospital.

Sandy Powell signs an autograph after opening Wrightington Hospital garden party in 1979.

Radio star Sandy Powell and his wife Kate White pictured with Norman Meadow.

Television and sporting stars enjoy a karting session with Wigan schoolchildren in 1988. They include Ian St John, Stu Francis, Sally Whittaker and Bill Beaumont.

Keith Chegwin presents his TV show from Wigan Pier in the late 1980s.

Ken Dodd opens a DIY store in Wigan in the late 1980s.

Ken Dodd with the Mayor and Mayoress of Wigan, Councillor and Mrs George Lockett.

Actor Edward Woodward and his wife, actress Michelle Dotrice, together with the widow of comedian Les Dawson when Mr Woodward was made honorary president of a Wigan brass band in the 1990s.

Ricky Tomlinson, formerly a star of TV's *Brookside* and more lately of *The Royle Family*, pictured at Appley Bridge boat rally in the early 1990s.

Pele, the great Brazilian footballer, signing autographs for fans when he came to open the JJB Stadium at Martland Mill in 1996.

By Royal Command

In 1954 the newly-crowned Queen Elizabeth II visited Wigan and as part of her visit she opened the John McCurdy Hall, now part of Wigan Tech. Here the Queen's motorcade travels along Market Street.

The Queen meets civic dignatories.

Press photographers try to get a decent picture of the Queen and the Duke of Edinburgh – not an easy task through the bobbing heads.

On her visit to Wigan in 1954 the Queen inspects local troops.

These Wiganers are at the bottom of Market Street, waiting for a glimpse of the new Queen who was paying her first visit to the town.

This little girl looks anxious as she waits for the Queen to arrive.

Flags at the ready, local children are well prepared for the royal visit.

Excited local children ready to fly their flags for the Queen.

Tea up! It's thirsty work waiting for a queen!

Local nurses wait to greet the royal visitor in 1954.

The Queen with local officials at the launch of the Three Sisters Recreation Scheme in the late 1960s.

The Queen Mother on her visit to the new H.J. Heinz Factory in Kitt Green, Wigan, in 1959.

The Queen meets local women during her visit to Wigan in 1977, her silver jubilee year.

Early arrivals at Wallgate for the Queen's 1977 visit to the town.

The Queen accepts a small bouquet of flowers during her 1986 visit to open the newly-refurbished Wigan Pier area in 1986.

Crowds are held back by barriers at Wigan Pier.

Always a dearly-loved figure, the Queen Mother
visits Wigan in 1959, and is seen here in the former
Wigan Council Chamber.

Princess Anne accepts a bouquet when she arrives to open a factory at Bryn in the 1980s.

Wigan workers chat to Princess Anne.

The Princess Royal visits
the Heinz factory in 1989.

The Princess of Wales has her hands full during the visit to Wigan in November 1991.

Now what shall I have…? The Princess of Wales seems to be deciding what to eat at Edward's bakery in Wigan Market Hall.

The Princess of Wales meets the Mayor of Wigan, the late John Horrocks, on her visit to the town in November 1991.

More Union flags at the ready to greet a royal visitor… and doesn't that young man look smart in his flat cap?

The Duke of York with members of Wigan Golf Club. He played a round on the Arley course and then attended the club's annual dinner in January 1998.

Subscribers

Margaret & George Aspey
Mr Nolan Aspey
Bache Family
Irene Banks
Colin Bean MA
Maureen & Ronnie Bentham
Ellen Berry
Jane Birchall
Marguérite E. Braddock
Audrey & Peter Calderbank
Mrs Emily E. Clark
Frank Clayton
John & Elizabeth Coalfield
Samuel H. Cox
Councillor George Davies
David & Pauline Leonie Derbyshire
Frank Dickinson
Mr John & Marjorie Disley
William Duckworth
Alice, Emily, Rebecca, Anne & Nicholas Fairhurst
Keith & Doreen Fanning
Connor James Farrimond
Geoffrey Foster
Cyril & Jean Fowler
Rebecca Gaskell
Stuart, Marina & Benjamin Gaskell
Tom & Phyllis Gaskell
Gilded Hollins C.P. School
Tom Gill
Gillian Gray, Editor, *Wigan Observer*
George Hamlett & Joan Hamlett
Kathleen Heaton
John Helsby
Joshua George Hesketh
Kevin Hesketh
Sheila L. Highton
Mary & Ronnie Hilton
Margaret Houlton
Joan & Derek Hughes
A. Hurst
Lynn Hurst
Mr James Hynes
Mrs Eunice James
Eric King
Mr A. Knowles
Mr P. Knowles
Mr Layland
Mrs Phyllis Lee
Elizabeth Lillian Lewis
Mr David Lewis
Catherine Lucas

Mrs Susan Lupton
Mr & Mrs D.J. McCormick
Belinda & Katie McDermott & Leanne & Staceylea Metcalfe
Chris McVeigh
W. Maggs
Mr & Mrs Harry Meadows
Thomas Merry (Wigan Mayor 1954)
Peter Miles
Ann Morgan
The Moss Family
Councillor John O'Brien
Mrs Hazel O'Brien JP
Kevin John O'Leary
Peter O'Neil
Mrs Mary O'Mara
Frank Orrell
Joyce Parker
Marjorie & Jeff Partington
Councillor William Pendleton
Mary Perry
Mrs Marjorie Peters
Margaret Plumpton
Edward Power
Mr & Mrs T. Purdhan
Brenda Purnell
Ian Rasburn
Francis K. Regan
Mary Robbins & Sheila Cunningham
Grandchildren of Winifred Rollins
Judy, Peter, Simon & Gareth Rowe
St Mary & St John Catholic Primary School
St Williams Catholic Primary School
Councillor George E.R. Seaward
Miss Millie Sharkey
Nora Sheridan
Carole Slater
Stuart Prior Smith
Councillor Brian Jerome Strett
Taffy
Mrs C. Taylor
Frank Thorley
Anne Agnes Topping
Gordan Peter Tyrer
Ann Elizabeth Twiss
John C. Vagon
Len Walls
Jenny Warburton
Mr & Mrs K. Werrill
Mr D. Williams
Mr James Wimsey

Printed in Great Britain
by Amazon

29897789R00108